Fables and
Fairy Tales

Simplified by Michael West

Revised by D K Swan

Illustrated by Clive Spong

Longman

500 word
vocabulary

Longman Group UK Limited
Longman House, Burnt Mill, Harlow,
Essex CM20 2JE, England
and Associated Companies throughout the world.

First published 1931
Second edition 1957 (19 impressions)
Third edition 1978
Twelfth impression 1989

ISBN 0-582-52544-6

Produced by Longman Group (FE) Ltd
Printed in Hong Kong

Contents

Words outside Stage 1 of New Method Supplementary
Readers are explained on p. 59.

Fables

1 The old cat

An old woman had a cat. The cat was very old; she could not run quickly, and she could not bite, because she was so old. One day the old cat saw a mouse. She jumped and caught the mouse. But she could not bite it; so the mouse got out of her mouth and ran away.

The old woman was very angry because the cat had not killed the mouse. She wanted to hit the cat. But the cat said, 'Don't hit your old servant. I have worked for you for many years, and I would work for you still, but I am too old. Don't be unkind to the old, but remember the good work that the old did when they were young.'

2 The city mouse and the country mouse

Once there were two mice. They were friends. One mouse lived in the country; the other mouse lived in the city. After many years the country mouse saw the city mouse; he said, 'Do come and see me at my house in the country.'

So the city mouse went. The country mouse took

him to his house in a field. He gave him the nicest food that he could find.

The city mouse said, 'This food isn't good, and your house isn't good. Why do you live in a hole in the field? You should come and live in the city. You would live in a nice house made of stone. You would have nice food to eat. You must come and see me at my house in the city.'

The country mouse went to the house of the city mouse. It was a very good house. Nice food was set ready for them to eat. But just as they began to eat they heard a great noise. The city mouse cried, 'Run! Run! The cat is coming!' They ran away quickly and hid.

After some time they came out. Then the country mouse said, 'I don't like living in the city. I like living in my hole in the field. It is nicer to be poor and happy, than to be rich and afraid.'

3 The man and the apples

A man was going to a rich man's house. As he went along the road, he saw a box of good apples at the side of the road. He said, 'I don't want to eat those apples because the rich man will give me a lot of very nice food to eat.' Then he took the apples and threw them away into the dust.

He went on and came to a river. The river had

become very big; so he could not go over it. He waited for some time; then he said, 'I can't go to the rich man's house today because I can't get over the river.'

He began to go home. He had eaten nothing that day. He began to want food. He came to the apples, and he was glad to take them out of the dust and eat them.

Don't throw good things away; you may be glad to have them at some other time.

4 The friends and the bear

Two friends were going through the forest. One friend said to the other, 'If any beast comes out from the trees, I'll stay with you and help you.'

The other friend said, 'I will help you too, if any beast comes out at you.'

After a little time there was a great noise, and a big bear came out from the trees. At once one of the friends ran and got up into a tree. The other friend was fat; he tried to get up into a tree but he fell down at the foot of the tree. There he stayed still.

The bear came near to him; it put its nose down and smelled him. It thought that the man was dead, so it went away.

The other man came down from the tree, and

said, 'What did the bear say to you when it put its
mouth so near to your ear?'

His friend answered, 'The bear said, "Don't go
with friends who run away from you when you
want their help most."'

5 The cat and the bell

There were a lot of mice in a house. The man of the
house got a cat. The cat killed many of the mice.

Then the oldest mouse said, 'All mice must come
to my hole tonight, and we will think what we can
do about this cat.'

All the mice came. Many mice spoke, but none
knew what to do.

At last a young mouse stood up and said, 'We
must put a bell on the cat. Then, when the cat
comes near, we'll hear the bell and run away and
hide. So the cat will never catch any more mice.'

Then the old mouse asked, 'Who will put the bell
on the cat?'

No mouse answered.

He waited; but still no one answered.

At last he said, 'It is not hard to say things; but it
is harder to do them.'

6 Mr Sparrow and Mr Fox

Not a nice little bird

Mr Sparrow was a little bird. He was not a nice little bird—not at all nice; he liked to tell stories about one person to another person.

One day, as Mr Sparrow sat in a tree, he saw Mr Rabbit coming through the forest. Mr Rabbit came near to the tree, and Mr Sparrow heard him speaking.

Mr Rabbit was saying, 'I'm going to do something which will make Mr Fox very angry! Ha! Ha! Ha! He will be very, very angry!'

Then Mr Sparrow cried out to Mr Rabbit, 'No, you will not! For I'm going to tell Mr Fox what you have said.'

Mr Rabbit thought, 'Now I don't know what to do. What shall I do if that ugly little Mr Sparrow tells Mr Fox what I said?'

Mr Sparrow went away quickly and told Mr Fox what Mr Rabbit had said. Mr Rabbit thought and thought; at last he said, 'I know what I shall say!'

'I'll hear you nicely'

In a little time Mr Fox came running along the lane. Mr Rabbit called out to him, 'Mr Fox, Mr Fox!'

'What?' said Mr Fox.

'Don't come near me,' said Mr Rabbit.

'Why?' said Mr Fox.

'Because you'll kill me and set my house on fire.'

'Why do you say that?' asked Mr Fox.

'Because I was told so,' said Mr Rabbit. 'I was told that you said, "I'm going to kill Mr Rabbit and set his house on fire."'

'Who told you that?' asked Mr Fox.

'It was Mr Sparrow.'

'It was, was it?' said Mr Fox.

The next day, Mr Fox saw Mr Sparrow in the forest. Mr Sparrow called out to Mr Fox.

'What do you want?' said Mr Fox.

'I have something to tell you,' said Mr Sparrow.

'You have, have you?' said Mr Fox.

'Yes, I have,' said Mr Sparrow.

'Stand on my head, little Mr Sparrow, because one of my ears is bad, and I can't hear with the other,' said Mr Fox.

So Mr Sparrow jumped on to Mr Fox's head.

'Stand in my mouth,' said Mr Fox; 'then I'll hear you nicely.'

Mr Sparrow stood in Mr Fox's mouth. Mr Fox shut his mouth and ate Mr Sparrow. 'Now go and tell stories about me!' said Mr Fox.

7 Mr Rabbit kills a wolf

The creatures of the forest
One day all the creatures of the forest came to one
place. All the big creatures came, and all the little
creatures came. There were horses and cows and
rabbits and foxes and ducks and mice and birds, and
all the other living things. They were very afraid.
For a great big wolf had come to the forest; and the
great big wolf had said, 'I'll kill you all if you don't
give me food three times every day.'

'What shall we do?' said Mrs Duck. 'What *shall*
we do?'

'What ever shall we do?' said Mr Fox.

'What shall we do?' said all the creatures.

'I know what we must do,' said Mr Rabbit, looking very big. 'We must kill this Mr Wolf. . . . And
I shall do it.' Then he walked away along the road
to Mr Wolf's house. All the beasts looked at him.

'What is he going to do?' said Mrs Duck. 'What
is he going to do?'

As Mr Rabbit went along the road, he saw a
well in a field. The well was full of water.

Then Mr Rabbit went on and came to a river. He
jumped into the water; then he walked through
some dust; then he jumped into the water; then he
walked in the dust again. And soon he looked a
very poor, ugly little rabbit, covered with water
and dust.

'It isn't hard'

At last Mr Rabbit came to Mr Wolf's house.

'Who are you?' said Mr Wolf.

'Please, I am your food for today.'

'You! You ugly little creature! Tell them to send me a big fat cow, or a horse, or a hundred fat ducks.'

'Please,' said Mr Rabbit, 'the other wolf wants all the good food. So we have sent him all the cows and the horses and ducks. We must give them to him, because he is bigger and braver than you are.'

'Oh, is he?' cried Mr Wolf. 'We shall soon see if he is! Come with me and show me where he lives.'

Then Mr Rabbit led Mr Wolf to the well in the field.

'He's down there,' said Mr Rabbit. 'Don't go near him or he'll kill you.'

Mr Wolf went to the side of the well and looked down. He saw his own angry face in the water. He thought that it was the face of another wolf looking up at him. He jumped down into the well to kill the other wolf. He fell into the water; and he could not get out.

Mr Rabbit went back to the other creatures. 'It isn't hard to kill a wolf,' he said, 'if you know how to do it.'

8 'Mr Fox is dead'

A plan to catch Mr Rabbit

Mr Rabbit sometimes did things that made other people angry, so that they wanted to catch him. But it was very hard to catch Mr Rabbit.

One day Mr Wolf said to Mr Fox, 'We'll catch Mr Rabbit and eat him tonight. You go to your home and get into bed. I'll say that you are dead. Then Mr Rabbit will come near you to look at you, and you can jump up and catch him.'

Mr Fox ran home and got into bed.

Mr Wolf went to Mr Rabbit's house. He stood at the door and called, 'Mr Rabbit, Mr Rabbit.'

'What is it?' said Mr Rabbit.

'Have you heard about poor Mr Fox? It is so sad!'

'No,' said Mr Rabbit, 'I haven't heard anything about Mr Fox.'

'He's dead!' said Mr Wolf.

Mr Rabbit gets away

Mr Wolf went away. Mr Rabbit went to Mr Fox's house to see what he could see. He looked in through the window, and there he saw Mr Fox on the bed with his eyes shut, looking like a dead fox.

Mr Rabbit thought, 'I must see if he is dead or not. Because if he isn't dead, he'll catch me when I go near to him.'

Mr Rabbit went into Mr Fox's house. He looked

at Mr Fox and said, 'Mr Wolf says that Mr Fox is
dead but he doesn't look like a dead fox. You always
know if a fox is dead, because dead foxes always
open their mouths.'

Mr Fox heard this, and he thought, 'I'll show him
that I am dead.' So he opened his mouth.

When Mr Rabbit saw Mr Fox open his mouth he
knew that Mr Fox was not dead. Mr Rabbit jumped up and ran out of the house as quickly as he
could.

9 Mr Rabbit and Mr Wolf

A great stone

One day Mr Rabbit was walking near the hill. He
heard someone crying out, 'Help! Help!' He looked
this way and that way, and he saw poor Mr Wolf.
A great stone had fallen on Mr Wolf's back, and he
could not get up. He cried, 'Mr Rabbit, take this
great stone from my back or I shall die.'

Mr Rabbit worked very hard and got the stone
from Mr Wolf's back. Then Mr Wolf jumped up
and caught Mr Rabbit in his mouth.

'If you kill me,' cried Mr Rabbit, 'I will never
help you again as long as I live.'

'You will *not* live,' said Mr Wolf, 'because you'll
be dead.'

'No nice person kills a person who has helped

him,' said Mr Rabbit. 'It isn't just. You ask Mr Duck; he is very fat and he knows everything. He will say that no nice person would do a thing like that.'

'I'll ask him,' said Mr Wolf, 'and if he doesn't say what I want, I'll eat him too.'

'Stay there!'
So Mr Wolf and Mr Rabbit went to Mr Duck.

Mr Wolf said, 'I caught Mr Rabbit when he was sitting down near the hill. So I say that I should eat him. Now say what you think.'

'I took a great big stone from his back,' said Mr Rabbit, 'so I say that he should not eat me, because I helped him. Now say what you think.'

'What stone?' said Mr Duck.

'A stone near the hill,' said Mr Rabbit.

'I must see it,' said Mr Duck. 'How can I say what I think if I haven't seen the stone?'

So Mr Wolf and Mr Rabbit and Mr Duck went to see the stone.

'Now, put the stone just as it was,' said Mr Duck.

So they put the stone back where it was.

'No,' said Mr Duck, 'that isn't just as it was. You said that the stone was on Mr Wolf's back.'

So they put the stone on Mr Wolf's back.

'Now,' said Mr Wolf, 'you see just how it was. What do you say about it?'

Mr Rabbit and Mr Duck said, 'We say that we

are going home. And you may ask some other person to take the stone from your back. You look very nice like that. Stay there!'

10 Mr Duck and Mr Rabbit

No money for Mr Duck
Mr Rabbit said to Mr Duck, 'Come and work with me, and you'll get more money than you have ever had before.'

Mr Duck said, 'I'll come.'

So Mr Duck worked with Mr Rabbit. After some time, Mr Duck said to Mr Rabbit, 'I want to buy some things. Please give me some of the money that we have got.'

Mr Rabbit said, 'Things have gone very badly. I have no money to give you now.'

Mr Duck knew that this was not true. He said to himself, 'Mr Rabbit has the money, but he doesn't want to give it to me.' But Mr Duck said nothing. He went away; and he thought and thought. He did not go to sleep at night, but stayed awake thinking. He was thinking how he could get the money from Mr Rabbit.

One day Mr Duck came to Mr Rabbit and said, 'I don't want that money now: I have found a great big hole near the river. It's full of gold. It's full to the top. I never saw so much gold. There's more

than I can take away; will you help me to take it
away?'

Mr Rabbit said, 'Yes, I'll be glad to help you.'

So Mr Rabbit and Mr Duck went down the road
to the river. When they came to the side of the
river, Mr Duck said, 'It's on the other side of the
river.'

Over the water

'How shall I get over the water?' asked Mr Rabbit.

'Sit on my back,' said Mr Duck, 'and I'll take you
over.'

So Mr Rabbit sat on Mr Duck's back, and Mr
Duck went into the water. When Mr Duck was a
long way from the side, he said, 'Now I'll go down
into the water, and you will fall from my back into
the water.'

'But that will kill me!' said Mr Rabbit.

'Yes,' answered Mr Duck, 'so it will. But you
didn't give me my money for the work that I did
with you.'

'I hid the money in a pot in my house. Take me
home and I'll give it to you,' said Mr Rabbit.

Mr Duck said, 'I'll take you home, and we'll go
to your house at once, and you can give it to me.'

So Mr Rabbit gave Mr Duck the money.

Mr Rabbit was afraid of Mr Duck after that.

11 The babes in the wood

A rich man's children

Once there were two little children. They lived with their father and mother. Their father was a rich man. He had a beautiful house and a large garden. Their mother was a nice woman, and she was very kind to the children. So the children were happy, and they loved their father and mother.

After some time their mother fell ill and died. Soon after that the children's father died too. So the two poor little children were alone; they had no father or mother.

The children's father had a brother. The brother was a bad man. When he heard that the children's father and mother were dead, he thought, 'My brother was very rich. He had a big house and a lot of money. I'll go and live in that big house. If his children die, all that money will come to me. I'll go and see what I can do.'

'Come with us'

So he went and lived in the house with the children. He was not kind to the poor children. He called them bad names and when they made any noise, he hit them.

He said to himself, 'I want these children to die. Then I shall get all the money.'

At last he sent for two very bad men. He said to them, 'I want these children to die, then I shall get all their money. Take them away into the forest and kill them. When I know that they are dead, I'll give you a lot of money.'

The two children were playing in the garden. The two bad men went out into the garden, and found the children there. They said to the children, 'Come with us into the forest. We have found a beautiful place where there are a lot of flowers. A bird has made a little nest in a tree there, and you shall see her eggs. Come with us and see the flowers and the little bird's eggs.'

The children said, 'Oh, yes! Show us the little bird's eggs!' They took the men's hands and went with them, saying, 'Come, come quickly and show us the eggs.'

So they went into the forest with the two bad men. They went a long, long way.

The children said, 'Is it far from here to the little bird's nest and the place where the beautiful flowers are?'

The men said, 'Not far—just a little way.'

They went on—and on. The children said, 'Is it far from here to the flowers and the bird's eggs? We are little, and we can't go far.' But the men went on —and on.

At last the children said, 'We can't go on any more. We must sit down here. We'll see the flowers and the little bird's eggs on some other day.'

Then one of the bad men said to the other, 'I don't like killing children; they are so small. Night is coming, and it's very cold. They are far from home; they can never find the way back. We'll go away, and they'll die here in the forest.'

The other man said, 'Yes, we'll do that.'

So the two men went away....

Alone in the forest

The two little children were alone in the forest. They ran this way and that way, but they could not find the road. At last they fell down at the foot of a big tree. They had no food; it was very cold. They sat at the foot of the tree and cried. And when they could not cry any more, they fell asleep, hand in hand.

The little birds came and saw them sleeping there. They said, 'Poor little children, they'll be cold through the long night.'

So the birds went and brought leaves; and they covered the little children with leaves.

Night came over the forest. And the little children slept, hand in hand, covered over with leaves. Bears and wolves came out; and there were angry noises in the night. But the little children slept hand in hand in their bed of leaves.

Day came into the sky and the birds woke up in the tree-tops. One little bird went down and stood by the children. 'Wake up,' he cried, 'wake up, little children. Day has come.' But there was no answer. The little children slept still, hand in hand, in their bed of leaves. Then all the little birds came down from the tree.

'They are sleeping,' said one little bird.

'They are dead,' said another. 'They will never again know night or morning, sunlight or rain; but they will sleep, and sleep always, hand in hand in their bed of leaves.'

12 Rumpelstiltskin

A very beautiful girl

Once upon a time there was a very poor man. He had one child—a girl. She was very beautiful, and she knew how to make very nice cloth.

The poor man was always saying, 'My girl is *very* beautiful. She makes cloth; the cloth is *very* beautiful.'

One day the King of that country came along the road. The poor man told the King about his daughter. 'She's very beautiful,' he said, 'and she makes beautiful golden cloth!'

'What does she make the golden cloth out of?' asked the King.

'She can make it out of anything. She can make golden cloth out of paper,' said the father.

The King loved money. He thought, 'I'll give this girl paper, and she will make golden cloth out of it. Then I'll get a lot of money for the golden cloth.' So he said to the poor man, 'Send your girl to my palace and I will see what she can do.'

So the girl went to the King's palace. He put her in a little room, and gave her a great box of paper, saying, 'Make all this paper into golden cloth.'

The girl said, 'I can't do it. I can make cloth, but I can't make cloth out of paper.'

'Your father said that you could make golden cloth out of paper.'

'My father is always saying things about me that aren't true.'

Then the King became angry, and said, 'Make that paper into gold cloth before morning, or....' He shut the door and went away.

The little man
The poor girl was afraid. She sat down and cried.

As she sat there, she heard a noise, and she looked up and saw a little man. She had never seen a man like him before. He was very small, and his face was very ugly.

The little man said, 'Why are you crying?'

'I must make all this paper into gold cloth, and I don't know how to do it.'

'What will you give me,' asked the little man, 'if I do it for you?'

'I'll give you this ring from my finger,' said the girl.

Then the little man sat down and began to work. He worked all night; and in the morning, when the King came, all the paper had become golden cloth.

When the King saw it, he was very pleased. But he wanted more gold. He called his servants and they brought another box—a bigger box—full of paper. Then he said, 'Now I know that you can do it. Make all this paper into cloth of gold before morning.'

The girl said, 'I can't do it.' But the King shut the door and went away.

'*Give me your little son*'
As she sat there the little man came again. He said, 'What will you give me to do this work for you?'

She answered, 'I'll give you these beautiful shoes from my feet.'

Then the little man sat down. He worked all night, and in the morning all the paper had become cloth of gold.

The King was very pleased when he saw it. He called his servants, and they brought more paper— much more paper. He said, 'If you make all this into cloth of gold before morning, you shall be my Queen.'

As soon as she was alone, the little man came in. 'What will you give me to make all this into gold cloth?' he asked.

'I have nothing more to give,' she answered.

The little man said, 'When the King marries you, and you become his Queen, you will have a little son. Give me your little son.'

'I may never have a son,' the girl thought. So she said, 'Yes, I'll do that.'

Then the little man sat down and worked all night; and in the morning all the paper had become cloth of gold. The King came in the morning and he was very pleased. He married the girl and she became his Queen.

'My name is . . .'

After some time the Queen had a son. She was very happy, and she did not remember the little man and what she had said to him.

One day, when she was sitting in her room, the little man came to her, and said, 'You must give me your son. You said that you would give him to me, because I made all the paper into cloth of gold.'

The Queen said, 'I'll give you all the gold that is in this country; but don't take my son.'

The little man said, 'I don't want gold. But if you can tell me my name in three days, I will not take away your child.'

She said, 'Is your name John?'

'No, it isn't.'

'It is James? William? Alfred? Timothy?...'
She said all the names that she could remember. But
it was none of them.

The little man said, 'I'll come again tomorrow.'

That night the Queen sent men into all the places
near to find out as many names as they could.

The next day the little man came again. The
Queen said all the names she could think of—
Frog-face? Fat-head? Ugly-nose?' But it was none
of them.

On the next day some of the men came back.
They told her a lot of names; but she had said them
all before; it was none of those. At last a servant
came to the Queen, and said, 'Last night I went up
a great hill. I saw a light far away. It came from a
hut on the top of the hill. I looked in through the
window and I saw a little man sitting in the hut.
And I heard him speaking. This is what he said,
*"The Queen doesn't know! The Queen doesn't know!
The Queen doesn't know—that my name is—my name
is Rum-pel-stilt-skin—Rumpelstiltskin!"'*

When the Queen heard this, she was very glad.

Soon the little man came.

The Queen said, 'Is your name John?'

'No, it isn't!'

'Is your name Bob?'

'No, it isn't!'

'Is your name Rumpelstiltskin?'

Then the little man was very angry. He cried, 'Some wizard has told you!'

Then he jumped through the window and ran away—and was never seen again.

13 The goose girl

The Princess

Once upon a time a king and queen had one child, a girl. The King died. Many years went by, and the girl grew up and became a very beautiful princess.

One day the Queen said, 'I am becoming very old; it is time that my child was married. The King of the next country is my friend, and he has a son— a very good prince. I will send the Princess to him. Then the Prince will see her and love her and marry her. When the King is dead, and when I am dead, they will be King and Queen of that country and of this country too.'

Then the Queen made ready many beautiful things—jewels and gold and beautiful clothes, and all that a princess should have when she is married— because the Queen loved her child very much. She gave the Princess a servant-girl too, to go with her and take her to the Prince. She got two horses, one for the Princess and one for the servant. The name of the Princess's horse was Falada. A great

magician had given Falada to the Queen: Falada
could speak.

The servant-girl

When the time came for the Princess to go away,
the Queen took a ring from her hand and gave it to
the Princess. 'Take this ring,' she said. 'You must
never lose it. It will save you from all unkind
persons and all bad things; it will help you
whenever you want help. . . . Be good, and you
will be happy. I may never see you again, because
I am very old, and soon I shall die.'

Then the Princess rode away, and the servant-
girl went with her.

The servant-girl was a very bad woman. She did
not want to be a servant; she wanted to be a
princess. One day, as they were riding by the side of
a river, the Princess said to the servant, 'Please get
down from your horse and bring me some water.
I want to drink.'

'No,' said the servant-girl. 'If you want to drink,
go and drink out of the river. I'm not going to be
your servant any more.'

The Princess did not know what to do. But she
wanted the water very much, and at last she got
down from her horse. She went down to the river,
and took the water in her hand to drink it. But as
she took the water in her hand, the ring fell from
her finger into the water, and she could not get it

back. The servant-girl saw this, and she knew that
the Queen's ring would not save the Princess from
her any more. The Princess came to Falada, her
horse, but the servant said, 'You can't ride on that
horse any more. That's going to be my horse. Put
on my clothes, and I'll have your clothes. You are
my servant now.'

Falada, the horse, said

> If your mother, the Queen, could see,
> How very sad she would be!

The old King

They went on. The Princess rode on the servant's
horse, and was dressed in the servant's clothes. And
so they came to the city of the King. As they came
near the city, the servant said to the Princess, 'If you
tell the King that I am not the Princess, I shall kill
you—I shall kill you with my own hands!'

They rode up to the King's palace. The Prince
was waiting at the door. He had never seen the
Princess; so he did not know her. He ran up to
Falada; he helped the servant-girl to get down from
the horse, and he brought her to the King. He told
the Princess to wait outside the palace—he thought
that she was the servant.

Now the old King looked out of the window and
saw the Princess waiting outside, and he saw how
beautiful she was. Then he went to the Prince, and

asked, 'Who is that beautiful woman waiting outside the palace?'

The servant-girl said, 'That is my servant-
woman. I brought her to be with me on the road.
Send her away and give her some work to do.'

The old King thought for some time. Then he
said, 'I don't know what work she can do. But I
have a boy who works with my geese and ducks.
She may go and help him. She'll be the goose girl.'

The name of the boy was Curdken.

The servant-girl was afraid of Falada. She knew
that the horse could speak, and she thought that
some day he would tell the King that she was not
the Princess. So she said to the Prince, 'My Prince,
please do something for me.'

'What is it?' said the Prince.

The servant-girl answered, 'My horse Falada is
not a good horse. Please tell one of your men to kill
Falada.' So the Prince told one of his servants to kill
Falada.

The horse's head

The Princess heard that Falada had been killed. She
went to the Prince's servant and said, 'Please do
something for me.'

The man said, 'I will.'

She said, 'I loved Falada very much, and now he
is dead. Please set his head on the wall over the door
so that I may see it as I go by.'

The servant did this.

The next morning, Curdken and the Princess went by the door. As the Princess came to the door, she looked up at the horse's head and said

> *Falada, Falada, where are you now?*

And the head answered

> *If your mother, the Queen, could see,*
> *How very sad she would be!*

Then they went out of the city and came to the field where the ducks and the geese were. A little river of clean cold water ran through the field. The Princess went to the side of the river and began to wash.

'Please go away,' she said to Curdken; but Curdken stood by and looked at her. Then the Princess said

> *Go, hat, go;*
> *Curdken's hat shall go;*
> *And after it shall Curdken go!*

Then Curdken's hat went away over the fields and over the hills; and Curdken had to run after it. When he came back, the Princess had washed. Curdken was very angry and would not speak to her. They stayed with the ducks and geese till night began to come; then they went home.

The next day the Princess looked up at Falada's head and said

> *Falada, Falada, where are you now?*

And the horse's head answered

> *If your mother, the Queen, could see,*
> *How very sad she would be!*

The Princess went to the river-side and began to wash, and Curdken stood by and looked at her. Then she cried

> *Go, hat, go;*
> *Curdken's hat shall go.*

Curdken had to run after his hat over the fields and over the hills; and, when he came back, the Princess had washed. Then they stayed with the ducks and the geese; and went home when night came.

Curdken tells the King

Each day it was just the same. At last Curdken went to the old King and said, 'I don't want that new girl to help me with the ducks and geese any more.'

'Why?' said the King.

'Because,' said Curdken, 'because she is always making me angry.'

'What does she do?' asked the King.

'When we go out in the morning she speaks to the head of a horse that is on the wall over the door. She says, "Falada, Falada, where are you now?" And the horse's head answers, "If your mother, the Queen, could see, how very sad she would be!"'

Then Curdken told how he had to run after his hat.

The King said, 'Go out again and I will come and
see what this goose girl does.'

The next day the King hid near the door; and he
heard the Princess speak to the horse's head, and he
heard what the horse's head answered. Then he
went to the field and hid in a tree. He heard the
Princess say, 'Go, hat, go!' Then he saw Curdken
running after his hat. Then the King went home.

The King sent for the goose girl, and said, 'I have
seen what you do. Tell me—why do you do these
things?'

Then the Princess began to cry, and she said, 'I
can't tell you. I can't tell anyone; because if I tell,
she will kill me with her own hands.'

But the King said, 'You must tell me. Nobody
shall touch you, but you must tell me everything.'

Happily ever after
At last the Princess told the old King everything.

Then the old King sent for the clothes of a
princess and made her put them on. When she had
put them on, she was so beautiful that he knew that
she was the Princess and the child of his friend, the
Queen. Then he sent for the Prince and the bad
servant-girl. And he sent for all the great men of the
city. They went into the big hall of the palace.

The King stood up and said, 'I have heard a story
of a servant-girl who took her Princess's horse and
her Princess's clothes, and made the Princess become

her servant.' Then he told all the story as it had been. At the last he said to the bad servant-girl sitting there, 'Now, what would you do to a person who had done those things?'

She answered, 'I would put her in a box and throw the box into the sea.'

The old King said, 'It was *you*! You did these things.'

Then they took the servant-girl and put her in a box, and threw the box into the sea.

The Prince married the Princess, and they became King and Queen of the two countries, and lived happily ever after.

14 The three beasts

A mouse, a donkey, and a bear

A man had lost most of his money. So he said to himself, 'I'll go away to some other country and begin again.' And he set out.

As he went along the road, he saw some children; they were making a great noise.

The man said to them, 'Why are you making that noise?'

'Look,' they said, 'we have got a mouse; see how he jumps and runs about!'

The man said, 'Poor little mouse, he's afraid. I'll give you some money and you can give me the poor little mouse.' Then he took the mouse, and put him in a field; and the little mouse ran away.

As he went along the road, he came to another place and saw some boys who had got a donkey. They were making it stand on two feet, and it sometimes fell down.

The man said, 'Poor donkey, it doesn't like walking on two feet. Give me the donkey and I'll give you some money.'

The poor donkey was very glad to run away. At another place some men had got a bear, and they were making it jump. The poor bear was very unhappy. So the man gave them some money, too; and the bear quickly ran away.

The man is saved

The man had now given away all his money. He came to the King's palace. He thought, 'The King has a lot of money. He can't be angry if I take a little of his money. I'll give it back to him when I get some money of my own.' He went into the palace and took some money. But, as he was coming out, the King's servants saw him. They took him to the King.

The King said, 'Put him in a box, and throw the box into the sea.'

The servants took a box; and they put in the box a bit of bread and a pot of water. Then they put the man in the box, and threw it into the sea.

It was a big box, and it was made of wood. So it stayed on top and did not go down under the water. After some time the man heard a little noise on the top of the box; and, some time after that, he saw a big hole. He put his head up through the hole, and there he saw the little mouse standing on the top of the box. The little mouse had bitten the hole through the wood. Then the donkey and the bear came and brought the box to the side of the water, and the man got out of the box. They had all helped him because he had been kind to them.

The Magic Stone

As they stood there beside the sea, they saw a white stone. It was a beautiful stone. Then the bear said, 'I know that stone. It's the Magic Stone. If you take it in your hand you will get whatever you ask.'

So the man took the stone in his hand and said, 'I want a big house and a beautiful garden and a lot of money for us.'

At once he saw in front of him a great big house with a big garden at the back full of flowers. When he went to the house, servants opened the door for him.

He lived in the house and was very happy.

Some time after that, three men came along the road. They said, 'How can this be? When we came here before, there was nothing here; but now there is this big house with a beautiful garden full of

flowers.' They wanted to know how the house and
the garden had been made so quickly. So they went
into the house and asked the man, 'How have you
made this house and this garden so quickly?'

He answered, 'I didn't make it. The Magic Stone
brought it.'

They said, 'May we see this stone?'

He brought the stone.

One of the three men took the stone in his hand.
As soon as he had got the stone in his hand, he said
to the stone, 'Take this house away to the city, and
take me and my two friends with it.'

There was a great noise, and the man found that
he was sitting by the side of the sea. The house and
the garden had gone. By his side was the box and
the pot of water and the bit of bread. And by the
box sat the mouse, the bear, and the donkey.

In the city

The bear said to the man, 'He has taken our house
away to the city. The city is on the other side of the
sea. You stay here, and we'll go and get the stone
and bring it to you.'

Then the donkey went into the water; the mouse
sat on the donkey's head, and the bear sat on the
donkey's back. Then the donkey swam over the sea
and came to the other side.

They found the house in the city. Then the bear
said, 'You go in, mouse, and see where the stone is.

You are small and no one will see you.'

So the mouse went into the house. He soon came
back and said, 'It will be very hard to get the stone.
It's in the room where the man sleeps. It's on a
table. On each side of the table there is a big cat
looking at the stone to see that no one takes it.'

Then the bear said, 'Wait; and when night comes,
go into the room and bite the man's nose.'

The mouse waited. When it was night he went
into the room. The man was asleep. The mouse
jumped on the bed and bit the man's nose.

The man woke up. He was very angry. He cried,
'Here I have two cats in the room, but a mouse bites
my nose! You cats do nothing!' Then he sent the
cats out of the room. After that he fell asleep again.

The fish help

The mouse jumped on the table. He got the stone
to the side of the table, and it fell down. He got it to
the door; then he could not get it along any more.
He called the bear. The bear put his foot into the
room and brought the stone through the door.
They went quickly to the side of the sea, where the
donkey was waiting. The donkey put the stone in
his mouth; the mouse got on the donkey's head;
the bear got on the donkey's back.

When they were near the other side, the bear
said, 'It was I who got the stone out of the house.'

The mouse said, 'No, I did it.'

38

The bear asked the donkey, 'What do you think?
Did I do it or did the mouse do it?'

The donkey said, 'The mouse did it, and you
helped.' But when the donkey said this, the stone
fell from his mouth into the water, and was lost.

Then the bear said, 'I know what we must do.'
He called the fish and said, ' A great beast is coming
to the sea to eat you all up. Bring me stones quickly
and I'll make a wall so that the beast can't come.'

Then all the fish were afraid, and they began to
bring stones. At last a very old and very fat fish
brought the Magic Stone; he was the King of the
Fish. The King of the Fish said, 'There! That is the
last stone in this sea. We can't find any more.'

The bear said, 'Thank you. The beast will never
come now; he has gone the other way. So you
mustn't be afraid any more.'

Then the man took the Magic Stone in his hand.
He said, 'Give me back my house again.' He looked
—and there the house was. Then he went into the
house; and the mouse, the bear and the donkey went
with him, and they all lived there happily ever after.

15 The golden goose

The little old man
Once there was a poor man who worked in the
forest. He had three sons. When the three sons grew

up and became men, he said, 'I can't give you food any more. You must work now and get your own money and food, because you are now men: you aren't children any more.'

So he gave the oldest of the three sons an axe, and said, 'Go into the forest and bring back some wood.'

The son took some bread and some water and an apple to eat in the forest; and he took the axe, and went to get wood. When he had gone a little way into the forest, he saw a very big tree. He thought, 'I'll cut this tree down and take wood to my father, to show what a big man I am and how hard I can work. I'll eat my food; and then I'll begin.' He sat down and began to eat the apple.

As he sat there he saw a little old man. The little old man said, 'Please give me a bit of your apple; I haven't had any food all day.'

The son said, 'No; go away. I can't give you anything.' The little old man said, 'Then I can't give *you* anything!' And he went away.

The son took his axe and began to work. But the axe did not hit the tree; it hit his foot. He could not stand or work any more; he had to go home.

The father was very angry when he saw that his son had brought no wood.

Inside the tree
The next day the father said to the next son, 'Today *you* must go into the forest and get some wood.

Your brother didn't help me at all.'

So this son took some bread and some water and an apple, and went to the forest. He came to the same tree, and sat down to eat his food.

The little old man came and said, 'Please give me a bit of that apple.'

The son said, 'No. Go away. Eat your own apples!'

The little old man said, 'I can't give you any-thing.' And he went away.

The son took the axe in his hands; but as soon as he hit at the tree, the axe hit his foot, and he had to go home.

The father was very angry. He said, 'See how my sons help me! They don't do any work at all!' The next day he said to his youngest son, 'Today *you* must go to the forest, and bring me some wood.'

So the youngest son took some bread and some water and an apple. He went into the forest and came to the same tree. He sat down to eat his food; and the little old man came.

The little old man said, 'Please give me a bit of that apple.'

The youngest son said, 'Take all the apple. I have this bread; I'll eat the bread.'

The little old man looked very pleased. When he had eaten the apple, he said, 'Hit the tree on this mark,' and he made a little mark on the tree. 'Soon you will see a great hole in the wood. Put your hand into the hole, and you will find something there which will help you.' Then he went away.

The youngest son did as the old man had said. As soon as he hit the tree with his axe, the side of the tree opened and he saw a great hole. He put his hand into the hole; he felt something hard and cold. He took it out and looked at it. It was a goose, made of gold. It was beautifully made—just as if it were alive.

The unhappy Princess

He thought, 'I will take this golden goose to the city. I'll sell it there and get a lot of money for it; and that will help my father.' So he went to the city, with the goose in his arms.

Now, in that city there was a king who had one child—a girl. The Queen had died, and the Princess was very sad. She never looked happy; but she sat all day and cried. At last the King said, 'If any man can make the Princess laugh, he shall marry her.'

The youngest son went along the street of the city with the golden goose in his arms. A girl saw the goose, and said to her friend, 'Look at that goose! Is it alive? Or is it made of gold? I must just put my hand on it, and see if it is alive or not.'

She went near and put her hand on the goose. Then she knew that it was made of gold. She thought, 'I'll see if I can take a little bit of the gold.' But she found that she could not take her hand

away from the goose. She had to run after the
youngest son, because she could not take her hand
away from the goose. She called to her friend,
'Come and help me; I can't take my hand away!'

Ha! Ha! Ha!
The friend came, and took the girl's arm. Then the
friend found that she could not take her hand away
from the girl's arm. So the girl's friend had to run
on after the girl and youngest son and the golden
goose.

An old man came along the street. He saw the
two girls, and said, 'Why are you two girls running
after that young man? Don't do it.' He put out
his hand and took the girl's arm. But he could not
take his hand away. So the old man had to run
after the two girls and the youngest son, and the
golden goose.

A fat man saw them and cried out to the old man,
'Why are you running after those two girls and the
young man? Come away!' He took the old man's
arm; but he could not take his hand away. So the
fat man had to run after the old man and the two
girls and the youngest son and the golden goose.

They went by the window of the King's palace.
The sad Princess was looking out of the window.
She saw the fat man and the old man and the two
girls all running after the youngest son and the
golden goose; and she cried out, 'Ha! Ha! Ha! I

never saw anything like it! Ha! Ha! Ha! Ha!'

The King heard this, and said, 'What has made
the Princess laugh?' Then he looked out of the
window and saw the youngest son. He called him
in, and said, 'You have made the Princess laugh
again. You shall marry her!'

So the youngest son married the Princess, and
they lived happily ever after.

16 John's wife and the fairies

The fairies
A man and his wife had two children. The man's
name was John.

John loved his wife very much; but she was not a
very good wife to him. She did not like hard work;
their hut was not very clean, and the children were
not very clean, and John's food was not always
nicely cooked.

John's wife slept in a room with the two children,
and John slept in another room. One night John
heard the children crying. He took a lamp and went
to their room to see why they were crying. His wife
was not in the room; and the door of the hut was
open.

The children said, 'We heard a noise; we woke
up, and saw a lot of little men in the room. They
were fairies. The fairies were dressed in white and

red clothes; they were as big as a man's hand. They stood all round mother, and called to her. She got out of bed and went away with them. She walked as if she were still sleeping.'

The cave

John ran out of the house and looked everywhere; but he could not see her. The next day, he asked a lot of people, but they had not seen her.

After some days an old woman came to John when he was working in the field. The old woman lived in a house near to John's hut. She said, 'I was just falling asleep last night when I heard a noise at the door. I opened the door, and just outside I saw a great big man sitting on a white horse. He said, "My wife and my child are ill. Come with me quickly and help her." Then he took me up on his horse. "Where are we going?" I asked. "You'll soon know," he said. Then he put his hand on my eyes; and when he took his hand away, I couldn't see anything. We rode on.

'After some time he took me down from the horse. He put his hand on my eyes, and then I could see. We had come to a great house. The door opened, and we went in. Inside the house there were great rooms full of beautiful things. We went through very many rooms, and at last we came to his wife's room. His wife was in bed. Her little child was with her, and the child was very ill.

'The big man kissed his wife and the child. Then he gave me a little box with a white powder in it. He said, "Rub that powder on the child's body." So I rubbed. As I rubbed, I put my hand to one of my eyes; and some of the powder went into my eyes. At once I saw everything changed. The beautiful room was not a room, but a great cave in the hill; the bed was a stone; and the woman and her child were poor ugly little things. I didn't like to look at them or to put my hand on them. But I said nothing.

'If John can catch me . . .'

'After some time the big man said, "Go to the door. I'll come soon." As I waited at the door, I saw your poor wife. She looked all round her, because she was afraid of the fairies. Then she said to me, "This is the House of the Fairies. They brought me here to help the Queen of the Fairies and her child. They want to make me stay here always—but you can save me. Each night all the fairies go down the lane to the river. I'll go with them. If John can catch me as I go by, I'll be saved."

'Just then the big man came and took me away on the horse. When we came to my house he gave me three bits of gold. I put the bits of gold on the table; but when I looked at them in the morning they were not gold, but three dead flowers.'

John said, 'I'll come with you to the lane tonight.'

'*Now!*'

That night they went to the lane. They stood at the foot of an old tree. Hours went by; but they saw nothing, and heard nothing. At last the old woman said, 'I can hear something coming from the river.' Then she said, 'I can see the fairies. There they are! Your wife is riding on the outside, so as to be near you as she goes by.'

John heard a noise like a lot of little things speaking, like birds far away. The noise came nearer. There were people going by; but he could not see who they were. Then the old woman cried, '*Now!*' John put out his arms and in his arms he saw his wife. Then the noise became very great. There was crying and calling. Little hands caught at his wife to take her away. Little hands hit him; little mouths bit him.

Then day began to come into the sky, and the fairies ran away. John had his wife in his arms. Her eyes were shut. He took her home; and she was very ill for many days. At last she opened her eyes. She got out of bed. Then she cleaned the house and washed the children.

John and his wife lived happily ever after.

17 The princess of the sea

An angry night

The King of Persia sat in his hall. There was a great
fire, for it was cold. The palace was on a hill near
the sea. The King got up from where he was sitting
by the fire, and went to the window. It was an
angry night outside; rain was falling and the sea
made a great noise at the foot of the hill.

As he stood there, he heard a cry, 'Open, O
King! Open the door!'

He went to the door and opened it. There he saw
a man; his eyes were blue—blue as the sea—and
when he spoke, it was like the noise of the sea. With
the man was a young girl; her face was white—
white as the sea-washed stones by the sea.

The man said, 'O King, take my sister; I have
brought her to be your servant.' He said this, and
went away quickly into the night.

The man had gone. The rain fell; it was an angry
night. The King saw at his door a little girl, alone.
He said, 'Do you want to be my servant?' But she
did not speak. 'Who are you?' he said. But she did
not speak.

Then he took her into the house. She became his
servant; she worked very hard; but she never spoke.

'I can never come back'

The girl grew up, and became a very beautiful

woman. The King loved her more and more. At last one day the King said to her, 'You are not a servant, but a princess, for your face is white—white as the sea-washed stones by the sea. Marry me and be my queen.'

She did not speak, but she took his hand.

So the King married her and she became his queen.

After some time the Queen had a child, a little boy. The King said, 'Now I am happy. One thing alone makes me unhappy: you never speak. Will you not speak to your child?'

Then the Queen took her child, and went down the hill to the side of the sea; and the King went with her. She took some little bits of wood and made a fire. She had in her hand a small box, made of gold. She took some powder from the box and threw it on the fire.

Then the King heard a great noise. The sea opened and very many men came out of it. One of the men came to the Queen. His eyes were blue—blue as the sea—and when he spoke it was like the noise of the sea.

He said, 'Will you come back now, my Princess, to the sea? You shall marry a King of the Sea, and be a Queen of great waters.'

Then the Queen spoke. She said, 'O my brother, I have married this King; and this is my child. I can never come back.'

Down the hill to the sea

The Queen's brother said, 'O King of Persia, there was a time when the men of another sea came into my country to take it from me. I was afraid that they would kill my sister. I knew that you were a good king; so I brought her to you to be your servant. I said to her, 'I'll bring you back to the sea when my country is my own again. Do not speak; you may speak when I come again.' Now my country is my own, and I want her to come back.'

But the Queen answered, 'No, I can't come back.'

Then the Queen's brother took the child from her arms. He jumped into the sea. The water went over his head; and they could not see him any more. They waited. After some time he came back. He put the child in the arms of the Queen, and said, 'He is a child of the sea. He lives in the water. . . . He will bring you back to the sea at last.'

Then the Queen's brother, and all the men with him, went away, down into the sea. . . .

Years went by. The King of Persia was very happy. His Queen spoke to him now, and he loved her more than ever. . . .

At last the King became old. He fell ill.

It was night. The Queen sat by his side. He opened his eyes and looked at her. 'I must go now,' he said. . . . He shut his eyes; he was dead.

Day was near. The Queen heard the noise of the sea at the foot of the hill, like great bells ringing. She took her son by the hand. And they went down the hill, hand in hand, to the sea.

Questions

1 THE OLD CAT
1 Why did the old woman become angry?
2 What did the cat tell the old woman to remember?

2 THE CITY MOUSE AND THE COUNTRY MOUSE
1 What did the city mouse cry?—'Run...'
2 Why did the country mouse like living in the country?

3 THE MAN AND THE APPLES
1 Why couldn't the man go to the rich man's house?
2 What was he glad to do?

4 THE FRIENDS AND THE BEAR
1 Why did the bear go away?—Because it thought...
2 What does a good friend not do?

5 THE CAT AND THE BELL
1 What did the young mouse say?
2 What did the old mouse ask?
3 Who answered?

6 MR SPARROW AND MR FOX
Not a nice little bird
1 Mr Sparrow was not a nice bird. Why?
2 What did Mr Sparrow hear Mr Rabbit say?

'I'll hear you nicely'
1 When will Mr Fox hear Mr Sparrow nicely?
2 What were Mr Fox's last words?

7 MR RABBIT KILLS A WOLF
The creatures of the forest
1 Why were all the creatures afraid?
2 Why did Mr Rabbit look a poor ugly rabbit?

'It isn't hard'
1 Mr Wolf said, 'Who are you?' What did Mr Rabbit answer?
2 How was Mr Wolf killed?

8 'MR FOX IS DEAD'

A plan to catch Mr Rabbit
1 What did Mr Wolf tell Mr Rabbit?

Mr Rabbit gets away
1 Mr Rabbit said, 'Dead foxes always...'
2 How did Mr Rabbit know that Mr Fox was not dead?

9 MR RABBIT AND MR WOLF

A great stone
1 What did Mr Rabbit do for Mr Wolf?
2 Mr Rabbit said, 'No nice person...'

'Stay there!'
1 What did Mr Duck want to see?
2 Where did they put the stone at last?

10 MR DUCK AND MR RABBIT

No money for Mr Duck
1 Mr Duck asked Mr Rabbit for some money. What did Mr Rabbit say?
2 Mr Duck stayed awake, thinking. What was he thinking about?

Over the water
1 'How shall I get over the water?' What was the answer?
2 Where had Mr Rabbit hidden the money?

11 THE BABES IN THE WOOD

A rich man's children
1 What happened to the children's father and mother?—They...
2 Who came to live with the children?

'Come with us'
1 What did he tell the two bad men to do?
2 What did the children want to see?

Alone in the forest
1 What did the children do when they could not cry any more?
2 What did the birds do?

12 RUMPELSTILTSKIN

A very beautiful girl
1 What could the girl make?
2 What did the King tell the girl to do?

The little man
1 What did she see when she looked up?
2 What did the girl give to the little man?
3 What did the little man do?

'Give me your little son'
1 The next day, what did the girl give to the little man?
2' What did the little man ask the girl to give him?

'My name is—'
1 When the little man came to the Queen, what did he ask for?
2 Where did the servant see the little man?
3 What did the little man do when the Queen said his name?

13 THE GOOSE GIRL
The Princess
1 Why did the Queen send the Princess away?
2 What was the name of the Princess's horse?

The servant-girl
1 What did the servant-girl want to be?
2 Where did the ring fall?

The old King
1 Where did the Prince tell the Princess to wait?
2 What work did the King give to the Princess?
3 What did the servant-girl ask the Prince to do to Falada?

The horse's head
1 Where did the servant put the horse's head?
2 What did the Princess say to Falada's head?
3 What did the head say?

Curdken tells the King
1 Who told the King about it?
2 Why was the Princess afraid to tell the story?

Happily ever after
1 What did the King ask the servant-girl?
2 What was done to the servant-girl?

14 THE THREE BEASTS
A mouse, a donkey, and a bear
1 What beast did the man save from the children?

2 What beast did he save from the boys?
3 What beast did he save from the men?

The man is saved
1 What did the man do in the King's palace?
2 Who made a hole in the top of the box?
3 Who brought the box to the side?

The Magic Stone
1 What did they find near the sea?
2 What did the man ask for?
3 What happened to the house?

In the city
1 How did the three beasts get over the water?
2 What did the mouse do to the man?

The fish help
1 Why did the stone fall into the water?
2 Who brought the Magic Stone?

15 THE GOLDEN GOOSE
The little old man
1 What did the little old man ask for?
2 What did the oldest son answer?

Inside the tree
1 What did the youngest son say to the old man?
2 Where was the golden goose?

The unhappy Princess
1 Why did the youngest son go to the city?
2 Why did the girl put her hand on the golden goose?

Ha! Ha! Ha!
1 What did the Princess do when she saw all the people behind
  the youngest son?
2 What did the King say to the youngest son?

16 JOHN'S WIFE AND THE FAIRIES
The fairies
1 How big were the fairies?
2 How did the children's mother walk when she went away?—
  As if . . .

The cave
1 Why couldn't the old woman see where she was going?
2 What did the man tell the old woman to do?

'If John can catch me...'
1 What do the fairies do each night?
2 What did the three bits of gold become?

'Now!'
1 Where was John's wife riding?
2 What did John see in his arms?
3 When did the fairies run away?
4 What did John's wife do when she got out of bed?

17 THE PRINCESS OF THE SEA
An angry night
1 Who sat in the hall?
2 What did the man with blue eyes say?

'I can never come back'
1 The King said, 'Will you not speak to your child?' Where did the Queen go then?
2 Who came out of the sea?
3 What did he say to the Queen?
4 What did the Queen answer?

Down the hill to the sea
1 He took the Queen's son from her arms. What did he do then?
2 What did he say when he gave the child back to the Queen?
3 What did the Queen do at last when the King was dead?

List of extra words

creature *a beast, bird, fish, or other living thing*
goose, (two) geese *see page 31*
laugh *make the noise (Ha! Ha!) that shows we are very happy*

leaf, (two) leaves

nest

palace *a king's house*
servant *a person who is paid to work in another person's house*

swim, swam
true *If Mr Brown says 'I'm a man', that's* true, *but if he says 'I'm a girl', that's* untrue.
well *a man-made water hole*

Set in Bembo 14/15½ pt.
Produced by Longman Group (FE) Ltd
Printed in Hong Kong